WEARING GREE.. & LIVING
THE DREAM

Cover & character edits done by the amazing,
@studentparamediclina
Find her on Instagram!

WEARING GREEN & LIVING THE DREAM

Jordan McDaid

About the author

Hailing from Co. Tyrone, North West of Ireland, I always found myself feeling unsettled. I found I got bored easily when I spent too much time in the one place or job. From the young age of 18 I uprooted and packed my case, working in various parts of Mallorca & the French Alps, gaining some valuable life experiences.

I returned home after a few years and fell into the 9-5. I hated it, I remember thinking, 'there has to be more to life than this', (Not to offend anyone in a 9-5 job, it just wasn't for me). Having worked abroad, living with strangers who became best friends, I knew I enjoyed the variety and...the unknown of things being temporary.

Fast forward a few short years of 'settled life', I moved to England simply to follow this dream career I had.
I remember when I first sparked interest in the career of a Paramedic, I began to follow a few Facebook groups. These groups were full of people with similar mindsets and those who had questions of the process in becoming a paramedic. So, remembering the guidance I found from those groups, I saw opportunity to share the experience of my journey to becoming a Qualified Paramedic.

To you, the reader.

I really hope you find this book helpful, in providing guidance and an insight into the process and some challenges faced as a Student Paramedic. I have aimed this at hopeful individuals who are questioning where to start in beginning their journey, I would love for these types of guides to be available in secondary schools and colleges, to give an insight into careers because honestly, how are we expected to choose a career for life without having a taste of it first?

I also just want to acknowledge that it is understood, careers in emergency care now have a huge audience and following, with the public now enlightened with various TV shows and documentaries, giving an insight into what the job entails. So, if you are reading this just for fun, I also thank you for your support!

Introduction

Never did I think I would start writing a book in the middle of completing my degree, perfect example of procrastination, right? But... we have found ourselves in the midst of a global pandemic so – now is a better time than any, surely! Let's get the boring stuff out of the way; Famous opening sentence - I've wanted to be a Paramedic for a l-o-n-g time. I worked in care whilst I was in secondary school and just knew I was good at it, I've always been told I'm a very caring person, good natured, I guess. I grew up as the eldest child/ Second eldest grandchild in my huge Irish family, so I've always helped out from a young age. Leaving school, I wasn't sure what I wanted to do, I just knew I wanted to sample life before I gave a career a thought, so off I went, worked in travel & hospitality abroad for a few years, on return I worked in Schools and day cares. It was from that, I learned that I loved working with people, of all ages, I found it so rewarding and I just love meeting people and hearing their stories!

If you're reading this book, you obviously have some interest in the same. You will know exactly what I'm talking about when I describe the feeling you get when you see or hear an ambulance fly by on blues? Or when you see the green team out in public... although it's a bad time for the person needing them, you find yourself getting excited as you catch a glimpse of the inside of the truck, you see all the equipment and how amazing the crew are at their jobs – That's a feeling I couldn't ignore; with that... I sat and made a plan;

how can I get myself to where I want to be?

'Your application has been unsuccessful'.

I explored all routes, firstly I explored applying through my local trust's recruitment for Emergency medical technicians. There was another guy from my town interested in applying also, so the two of us attended a written assessment day. We had to complete a written driving test, with 12 minutes to complete it. Impossible when I think back on it. We were both unsuccessful at the first hurdle.

I was gutted, mostly because I knew how long it will be before the trusts next recruitment, but I decided not to give up, I knew this was the career for me, so I explored other avenues.

This is when I applied for university, (at this stage I had been out of school for a few years - so navigating through UCAS was like a degree in itself!) I had to widen my search to England, as along with many things, N. Ireland was behind the times and did not offer Paramedicine as a University degree (Although that has changed now).

So, I done my research, filled out my application (only applying to one university) and a few weeks later, I received an interview invitation.

When the time came, I flew over and spent the weekend. On the day of the interview, I was a bag of nerves. However, I composed myself, and walked into a room full of hopeful individuals.
We had to complete a group activity before being interviewed separately. My interview started off well, I felt, but a few questions through me off. I simply did not prepare enough. When I arrived home a few days later, I received the dreaded but expected news that I was unsuccessful.

After sulking for a few days, I took a notion to ring some Uni's and enquire about the clearing process. Clearing is available to anyone who hasn't received any offers for their chosen course (so don't feel like your chances are all gone if you don't get offers initially). I literally went down the list of uni's alphabetically, to see which still had places available.
To my surprise, I was in luck, and one university offered me a telephone interview for the next day.

This interview felt more relaxed, probably because it was a conversation on the phone, but I felt I had loads to say for each answer, I was pleased that following the interview, I was offered a place over the phone. It was as easy as that (with the appropriate answers of course).

As you can imagine I was delighted, but I was also fecking shitting it... It was real then, I'd be packing up my life and moving to England in a matter of months, to a city I'd never been to and to people I'd never met. Was I sure I wanted this? But anyways, before I knew it, I was there.

My tips for attending an interview:

Do your research! About both the Uni and the profession.

Make a list of topics you've researched; this will help you feel organized and avoid missing anything important.

Arrive in good time, I'm not saying turn up the day before, but you know… just don't look rushed!

Compose yourself, by either some grounding techniques, breathing exercises or meditating, you know what works for you.

Relate answers back to yourself, and your experience, even if your previous jobs aren't in the same sector, there is still skills and qualities enhanced, link those to being a paramedic.

Ask questions! You may get the chance to ask questions at the end, It is a chance to show off your preparation if you can ask them something you know is going on in the particular area.

Most importantly, be yourself! Don't stress it, they liked you enough to give you an interview, so you're doing something right. Interviewers expect you to be nervous, so don't worry if you appear it. The important thing is, that you leave afterwards knowing you have said everything you wanted to. So, if you get flustered, take a breath and start again, ask for the question to be repeated if you like.

You got this!

The fun starts here.

My course started in January, and by the end of February, we were sizing up for uniforms and practicing ILS (Intermediate life support) - this involves fitting an airway whilst administering CPR to a patient, an essential skill which would equip us to at least contribute something should we come across this situation whilst in practice.

This, along with other skills such as patient assessment, primary/ secondary surveys and history taking were the key capabilities we were required to achieve from our first-year placements. Sounds simple enough, but when you are faced with a challenging patient or environment, asking simple questions and getting adequate answers from patients is a real skill at times!

Luckily, Uni didn't throw us straight in at the deep end in terms of exposure to practice. They arranged our first placements to be 2 weeks in a residential care home, followed by 2 weeks in a special needs school setting. I know what you are thinking, even the staff on both sites asked us daily, 'What's a paramedic student doing here?', basically, we were there to develop our communication skills. It was brilliant.

Learning and observing how people across the age range overcome daily barriers both verbally and physically. Amazing people!

Not long after this, we spent a few days training with the local Fire & rescue service. This was a real action-packed week, we got to cut open cars, extract each other from them and work together on scenarios they had planned which we may face in practice.

It was all so interesting and interactive, I almost changed careers that week...... almost.

Following this, we had lots of practice days in Uni, both individual and in group work, to learn anatomy and physiology, scenario situations (in which we even used the drama students to behave as patients) and basic observations.

We had to complete OSCE's. In life support, patient assessments and major incident scenarios.
These were completed in exam conditions and we received grades & feedback for our performance.

Similarly, we also had to pass a manual handling assessment to enable us to undertake lifting and carrying safely, whilst out on placement.
This involved lifting a weighted mannequin attached to a stretched and holding for 30 seconds. Then carrying the same mannequin up and down stairs using a carry chair.

With these assessments completed, and a foundation of knowledge implanted, I was preparing myself for my first ever ambulance shift, a 12-hour nightshift on the Rapid response vehicle (RRV) – exciting!

Back to you

If you have managed to secure a place at a University or on a Student Paramedic course, firstly,

CONGRATULATIONS!

Now, you are probably wondering what you can do in preparation. Well...

I would strongly suggest getting a good foundation on human anatomy and physiology! This was a huge module in our first year, it is obviously really important for a paramedic to know the human body inside out – literally. It will also favor you when you come to practice, and you are able to tell an arse from an elbow! (Seriously, I can think of one or two people who would struggle with that.)
I found the A&P colouring books useful, and YouTube videos, something different from just reading constantly!

I would recommend getting to grips with some medical terminology as well, look at the Glasgow Coma Scale (GCS) and learn it if you can, It is used to assess a patients conscious state and is given in every handover we do.

Equipment wise, don't go overboard. You can usually get things like pen torches, fob watches at your station, but if you would rather get your own, that's cool.

Invest in a good Stethoscope. These will cost around £80-£100, but should last your whole career.
I'd also recommend getting a manual BP cuff cheap off the internet, start practicing those manual BP's with your new shiny Steth!

Boots? I question boots as some Universities are good enough to provide them with uniform, so check with yours. If you do decide to still get your own, be careful as some universities and trusts will not cover you if you have an accident and you are not wearing Uniform issued boots!

Fitness – Work on your fitness, most trusts require a fitness test before allowing you to complete manual handling on the road, each trust is different, but work on things like carrying weights, grip tests and cardio, you want to perform at your best.

Now, imagine you're a few months into your course, you are preparing for your shifts and you are not sure what to pack...

A sports bag, or a hold-all size bag which allows room for your hi-vis, spare uniform, helmet, notebook, lunch, snacks! Honestly, a Mary Poppins sized bag, 'cause you will eventually fill it with all sorts.

SNACKS! Cup-a-soups, biscuits, anything that you can keep in your bag, if you are diverted from your break and you feel yourself getting hangry, you don't want to be dreaming of your lunch that you left in the fridge.

I would also say, Sunglasses, spare uniform, deo (some job's get sweaty!). Charger/ battery pack, a notebook for reflections and an extra layer if it's cold.

THE JOBS

Some jobs described have been changed slightly to maintain patient confidentiality. No dates, areas or names have been disclosed and some genders/ ages have been changed to protect patient's identity and dignity.

'You'll never forget your first job'.

I showed up for my shift extra early so I had the chance to meet my mentor, introduce ourselves and be shown around the station. My mentor was cool, it was a relief to see he was around the same age as me (considering he wrote his emails like an old man!) so I knew we would get on fine. I was allocated to work from a fire station which was shared with the ambulance service, pretty cool to have both emergency services housed under the one roof. (and let me tell you, those fire staff have comfy digs! Reclining seats whilst on standby? Don't mind if I do!)

We were not sat too long before our first call came through on the radio. Catagory 1 (Highest priority) – Adult female - Seizing, 2 miles away. We jumped in the car and my mentor switched on the blues '999 mode activated', My hands were sweating as we flew past the traffic, most part spent on the opposite side of the road – this is, so cool.

We arrived first on scene to a house, the patients parents met us at the door, they explained to us the patient is their daughter, in her 30s, known epileptic but had been seizing longer than what was normal for her. She was laid on her side on the sofa, noisy breathing from aspirating (Inhaling vomit into her lungs) and still seizing.

We pulled her from the sofa onto the floor to gain full access to her, attaching the monitoring equipment, checking oxygen saturations and inserting NPA (Nasal airways), we administered high levels of oxygen to help her breathing and allow us to use our suction machine to clear any vomit from her airway. Soon after, our backup crew arrived. (Control will always send multiple vehicles to a Catagory 1 if there are resources available). The paramedics on scene attempted to gain IV access so they could administer drugs, but this proved difficult, our next option was to IO this patient. (IO stands for Intra-ossculous, meaning the cannula is placed into the bone. It is done using a small drill which penetrates the bone allowing drugs to be administered directly into the blood flow). We cut off the patients' trousers and my mentor explained to the patient's parents what he was going to do (before they heard a drill and thought what the hell is going on). He IO'd her just below the knee, proximal tibia. Success, drugs administered, the patient stopped seizing. Result. We now had the tricky job of formulating a plan of extracting our patient on a scoop board. The trolley bed wouldn't fit in through the doorway, the living room which we were in was at an angle, we ended up navigating through the whole downstairs floorplan to remove this patient and get her onto the bed outside the front door. Once onto the ambulance, we pre-alerted the hospital and were on our way.

First job done, what could be next?

'the bread & butter of the job'

Call to a 79-year-old Female with Abdominal pain

The information we got on the way to this call was: Lady had onset of epigastric (lower) pain the previous evening. Worsening overnight, reports vomiting x3 and x1 episode of black stool.

On arrival, this patient was lay in bed, upset and visibly in pain. She was holding her stomach while she told us of her history. We follow a structure with our questioning for calls like this, the structure I find most helpful is OLDCARTS. Standing for:

Onset – When did this complaint start?

Location – Show me where exactly the pain/ complaint is?

Duration – Is it there constantly or does it come and go?

Characteristics – Describe the pain to me? Sharp? Dull? Ache?

Aggravation – Does anything make it worse?

Relief – Does anything make it better?

Treatment – have you taken anything to treat this complaint?

This structured way of questioning helps us to gain all the relevant information as part of our assessment, following this, I took out my stethoscope and had a listen to her tummy, bowel sounds present – a good sign, no blockages. I then felt her stomach, feeling for any lumps, bumps or abnormalities. No bulging masses observed. Her tummy was nice and soft although the patient described her stomach is more distended than usual.

Decision made, it is unclear what the problem is here, without the correct imaging and labs for tests, the best we could do was make this lady comfortable enough for the journey to hospital. IV access achieved and 5ml Morphine given along with IV paracetamol, the lady seemed a lot more at ease and we made our way, comfortably, to hospital.

Elderly patient – Fall

An elderly lady living alone, has had a fall on their way to the bathroom. The description reads 'Can't get up'.

The patient has pressed their emergency alarm which has dispatched us, we arrive to a block of flats and a downstairs neighbor greets us, they've heard the patient bang the floor using her walking stick for attention.

As we enter the flat, the patient is sat upright, against a wall in her doorway/hallway. It was a challenge as we could barely open the door due to the patient's position, we squeezed through.

I first inspected the injury, pain in hip, leg shortened and rotated. It was pretty obvious this was a left NOF (Neck of femur) fracture. The patient gave a pain score of 8/10. Again, this was another situation where we could only make the patient comfortable enough to be moved. Some oral paracetamol and an IV cannula inserted to give Morphine. Once we had her pain under control, we could think about moving her. Ambulances carry a special inflatable lifting cushion. We were able to use this to bring the lady up to chair height, then she slid across to the carry chair. We attached tracks to the chair as we had to face 2 flights of stairs. Tracks allow the chair to glide slowly downstairs rather than lifting over each step.

On route to hospital, and with the patient now comfortable, talks turn to her life, she explains she is a retired schoolteacher, she tells us she loved teaching and that she never had any children of her own. I truly think the best part of this job is meeting people from all different backgrounds, I love hearing people's stories.

Unconscious male – not breathing.

Its 0700am. Lights and sirens flashing through the morning city traffic. We arrive at an industrial estate and stop at a factory.

I grab the equipment, defib and suction machine, and dash in behind my mentor.

We are led to the bathroom, my mentor has the first glance in, however I take one look around me and realize, no one is trying to help? Everyone is quiet.

I look in the cubical and understand why.

This man has been dead for some time.

He's laid on the floor, rigor mortis has set meaning he is stiff in the position his body fell in.

He is, obviously dead.

We don't intervene as we recognize the signs that life is extinct. Instead, we step away and close the door over to keep the man's remaining dignity.

It is explained to us that the patient (deceased), did not turn up for his shift that morning, so when staff tried calling him, they heard his phone ringing from the bathroom.

Sadly, the poor man never made it home after his previous shift. He suffered a heart attack whilst on the toilet, presumably, the previous evening.

In cases like this, where a death has happened in a semi-public place, the police attend. The atmosphere is quiet, it's sad, obviously. His workmates talk amongst themselves.

I have so many questions, but I remain professional and save them for after. Did he have family? Weren't they expecting him home? Why does death happen so quick, without warning?

As harsh as it sounds, our assistance is not needed here, the coroner was contacted to remove the deceased and so, we are freed up for the next job.
I can't say my mind freed up as quickly, I carried that man in my thoughts rest of the day.

My next shift is a night shift, it's been quiet. Only 2 call outs so far, but towards the early morning, as the end of shift approaches and I'm dreaming of my bed... a call comes through, 'knife injury, blood loss'

Blimey – We ask control for some more information on this one, we have to consider was this an attack? Is the scene safe? Control radio in and tell us we're going to a house, were an elderly man has dropped a knife on his foot while making a sandwich. – Well, that's a relief.

We arrive to a bungalow. The patient's son greets us at the door, the patient is sat in the living room/bedroom (his bed is in the living room of the house), on his bed, and sure enough, there is blood everywhere. They have done a decent job at wrapping the foot in tea towels and every type of material. It must come off so we can have a look at the damage, but before we do, we want to see the knife that injured.

The patient shows us a whole collection of knives, beside him in his bed. When I say knives here, think huge, sharpened, butcher knives, that shine like they belong in a high-end hospitality kitchen.
'Ermmm.. ok, why are they in bed with you? And why are you using such knives to make a sandwich...at 5.50am?,' I ask.
The patient explains he used to be a fish monger, and that his collection of knives are his pride and joy. He spends most of his day in bed and enjoys sharpening them, daily.

Fair enough.

This morning, he has sat on the side of his bed, cutting gammon on his bedside table, to make sandwiches for his son who is going to work, when the knife has dropped off the table and pierced his bare foot. The knife did not stick, instead it bounced off and onto the floor, leaving the wound open.

We unwrap the packaged foot and have a look, blood is spurting from the wound. The knife has hit an artery. I clean the area around the wound, take a measurement and then wrap the foot up again, this warrants a trip to hospital. We package the man onto our chair and transfer him.
He's a hardy bloke, shows no sign of pain. Declines pain relief. He's full of stories, I enjoy listening to them on the ride in.

I often think of this patient when I drive past the area, I find myself wondering if he is still sharpening his knives every day, or if he now at least wears shoes while making sandwiches!

111 referral, Palliative patient – Shortness of breath

If you're not sure what palliative is, it essentially means the person is near the end of life & receiving care to keep them comfortable until they die. They often have reached the final stage of disease, where treatment is no longer working.

In this case, the patient was an older lady, who was diagnosed with an aggressive form of breast cancer only 1 year ago, and it has now spread to her lungs.
This lady was living in her home, alone, but her daughter lives nearby and checks in with her throughout the day. Her daughter found her this morning to be short of breath so called 111, who sent us.

As we walked into the room, I could tell this lady looked exhausted, she was frail and looked almost like she had made peace with her destiny in this situation. She was lay in her hospital bed in her downstairs living area, the bed is situated by the window overlooking her beautiful garden with un-spoilt views of the countryside. Was this window her only connection with the outside world in her final stage of life? I was carrying out my observations and doing a respiratory assessment on this lady, using my stethoscope to listen to her chest, when she whispered into my ear:

"I just want to die."

Not knowing what to respond to that with, our eyes made contact. I placed my hand on hers and gave it a squeeze. This is not what you want to hear from your patient who you wish you could do more for, but from what I understood, this lady had completely came to terms with her illness, and at 82 years old laying in her living room, on a hospital bed, I could totally understand her want for a peaceful death already, she has had enough.

We took our time on this call, contacting relevant services to try and get a plan in place for this lady's comfort.

Calls like this, amid the fast pace which we normally go at, just puts everything into perspective.

Death is often portrayed as this scary thing who no-one wants to meet, yet it is the one thing that is guaranteed to all of us who live. Some, like this lady, wait peacefully on their time to pass, and others don't know their time is near at all. This... is life.

'59-year-old female – suicidal'

When this call came through, my mentored turned to me and said, 'This job is yours', he was leaving the whole thing, to me.

Ok, I thought, I got this. I take out my phone on the way and I quickly researched ways of dealing with someone expressing suicidal thoughts.

We arrived at a supported living accommodation. We met our patient in her bedsit. She was crying, looked to be struggling, but she seemed accepting of help as she called 111, who sent us.

I introduced myself and my mentor that day. I asked the patient what has happened for her to call us today. She explains she has been feeling low for a while now, having recently moved to the accommodation she is in she feels she doesn't fit in well.

She explains she is known to crisis and mental health teams. When asked if she had taken anything or harmed herself today, she denied. Stating that she just didn't know what to do as she feels so low.

When asked why she had contacted 111 instead of the crisis team, she replied that they always tell her the same thing, we persuaded her to call them to speak to someone, when she got through, she turned on speaker phone and the crisis team told us to leave, they would take it from here.

Looking at the history on our system for this patient, she has had ambulances out 32 times in the past year for similar incidents. Mental health teams have also noted that she has not been engaging with their support. We left after speaking with the staff in the home who ensured us they would keep a close eye on her.

I found myself quite useless in this situation, I find it sad how many mental health cases the ambulance service attend, even though our toolkit for these types of jobs is empty, we provide the treatment from within ourselves. I wish we could do more, but I settle in knowing that this patient is known to the correct services and I hope she engages in their support.

33-Year-old female – seizure

The information from the caller: '33-year-old with autism living in supported living for learning difficulties, had a tonic colonic seizure for the first time in 7 years.'

This patient was in recovery from her seizure when we arrived, sleepy and lay slouched on the sofa. This gave us a chance to speak to her carers and find out what happened leading up to the seizure, along with how long it lasted. They were able to tell us our patient has autism and was living in supported living the past 10 years. They then stated that this was her first seizure in 7 years.

As she started to wake up, she became agitated, hitting, spitting, biting head banging, and slapping. She could not be consoled by anyone, she slid onto the floor and began banging her head off the tiles. When we tried to intervene, she would hit out.

The lady had urinated herself during her seizure and staff stated this was the second time she was incontinent and that this was not normal for her, nor was this aggressive behavior.

We queried Urine infection, as a possible cause for her seizure. Whilst trying to change the lady out of her wet clothes, she continues to remain agitated and has managed to smack one paramedic in the face, knocking his glasses off his face. The carer's repeat that the patient's behavior was totally unlike her usual self as described by her care team. Although this type of behavior is common following a seizure, she was becoming a danger to herself and others, so the decision was made to place her in safe holds, under the mental health act for her own safety and ours, whilst we transferred her onto the trolley and ambulance. Once on the ambulance we released her from safe holding, she quickly flung her arms and legs out of the straps, head banging against the head of the trolley and then began to spit and wretch vomit in her hands and throw it around the ambulance. We applied further PPE (Apron, googles) to minimize the risk of any bodily fluids being exchanged. We had to use safe holds as we transferred the patient into A&E as it was unsafe for her coming out of the belts on the trolley. The paramedic is at the top of the trolley and I am at her legs, holding her tight so she can't kick them out of the belts. I am in the firing line for the flying vomit and spit, my mentor smiles as he sees the moment I release he has chosen his position carefully.

We phoned ED ahead to let the hospital staff know we were coming as she will need a cubicle straight away.

Next up,

'Groin pain'

Groin pain can be serious enough, you have several main arteries that run through your groin, so pain in those could be a sign of problems in the Cardiovascular system.

This call though, turns out to be a nasty infection in the groin. Let me paint a picture: Boarded up flat, concrete floor, red lightbulb, no furniture only a mattress on the floor, disused needles and dog food cans laying around - poor dog.

Have you guessed it yet?... A drug den. We barely step foot in the 'door' when our scene safety instinct kicks in, 'Lets get you out to the ambulance to assess you then' we say.

The back of an ambulance may be small but at least it is clean and well lit. You appreciate it in situations like this. The lady is in her late 50's, she is an IV drug user, she has been injecting whatever substance into her groin and it has now become infected.

I take a look, the area is black in colour, the skin is beginning to rot, and the smell... let's not go there.

The lady looks to be in so much pain, understandably. She is going to need some strong IV antibiotics and probably surgery. We strap her in and attend the ED.

<u>Category 1 – Choking.</u>

This call comes through and the address is outside a general hospital. We are confused at first, but soon realise, that this particular hospital doesn't have an A&E.

We arrive and the patient Is sat in his father's car, he is holding his neck and is struggling to breathe. His father explains that he was eating steak and began to choke.
We take him on board the ambulance and administer back slaps, to no effect. The man is actively choking and coughing, but that is a good sign, coughing means air entry. After a few more attempts of back slaps and thrusts, we close the doors and switch on the blue lights. On the way to hospital, I make a pre-alert call.
There are some road works on the way in, meaning the road is uneven and we hit a bump. The food dislodges from the man's throat along with vomit and other lovely contents.
Result!
The man is relieved, as are we.

 Job done.

'Adult female, seizing.'

At this stage, I have been to quite a few seizures, so on arrival to this one I felt like I knew what needed done. However, by the time we had arrived the patient had stopped seizing and was now in a state of recovery, the sleepy state. She was lay on the sofa whilst her son filled us in on what happened. He explained that his mum has lung cancer which has now also spread to her brain, and that she was sent home with a few short months to live.

They have no plan in place if she deteriorates and no package of care organized, so we get on the phone. We start with GP's, get them to contact district services and arrange a call out to have the lady assessed and to form a plan with her family as to what steps to take next.

This all takes time, of course. So as the paramedic is doing that, I am sat with the patient and her son, she is awake now but remains tired, she is curled on the sofa. I can tell her and her son have a great relationship. He explains that he panicked and didn't know what to do when she became unresponsive. This whole experience really scared him.

This was an emotional job, a young family, her son was around my age, I dread to think how scary it is for him to know his mum might not see the end of the year. Soon after we arrived, his sister & her partner turned up as well. They were such a loving family, laughing and crying together.

We didn't leave until we had confirmation that the loose ends had been tied together and that this lady was now made known to the relevant support services. This was the best we could do for this patient and her family.

'Police assistance required.'

It was 8.30am when a call came through and we were only a minute or two away. Myself and my mentor arrived on scene. The scene in this story, is a public road on a busy rush hour morning. The call had come from a driver who was concerned about the driver in front of them, says they were driving erratically and are now slouched over the steering wheel. We investigate the car in question, and sure enough the driver is as described, a young man, late 20's. He looks like he has just woken up from a nap… or a seizure. He is foaming at the mouth, intoxicated? We will soon find out. I open the driver door and introduce myself, He looks spooked, like he does not know where he is. He tries to shut the door, but I am stood in the way. I take the keys from the engine. He does not even notice. I step back and he shuts the door. I go around the passenger side and explain to him who we are, and that we are concerned about him. He becomes ecstatic, hyper, crying, agitated. A whole mix of emotions and reactions playing out. He reaches over and tries to shut the door again, At this stage, my mentor has called for back-up, we need an extra crew, and police to control the traffic around us. The guy takes a liking to me and lets me test his blood sugars – they are within normal range. Our backup crew arrive, and the patient gets out of his car, he is over 6 foot tall, built, and he's chaotic. He is red in the face and sweating profusely. He has now noticed that we have taken his keys and he is not happy about it, there is no talking to him. He is not taking on anything we say. He is quite clearly under the influence. He jumps in and out of his car tearing the place apart looking for his keys, then he cannot remember what he is looking for. He assaults one of our crew. The car is rocking with his movement. We decide to lock his doors until the police arrive. He tries kicking out the windows and shakes the car violently. The sight of the police uniform is enough to calm him down, they cuff him, and we board the ambulance for further assessment. Once settled, he tells us he has taken cocaine this morning, on top of alcohol. He's taken it as he is under stress at work he explains, sorrowfully. He explains he was on his way to work this morning, I wonder is this his normal breakfast cocktail or if today was a one off.

His behavior prior to police arriving was a classic example of cocaine toxicity, where people find immense strength in rage and hyper behaviors, their body can't recognize its limits, it can be fatal.

I attach the ECG monitoring equipment and his heart is racing at 147 bpm. He is taken into hospital for monitoring. We find out later he is charged with assault, driving under the influence and driving without insurance. What a way to start the week, and I'm sure, an awkward phone call to the boss!

Saw accident.

With the first lockdown in the UK, came the motivation of people to carry out home DIY and work on home improvements. On this occasion we were called to a young man in his 20's who was cutting home shelving in his shed using a circular bench saw... you guess where this is going, right?

He's called 999 today after his glove caught in the spinning saw, by the time he hit the emergency stop, the machine had eliminated one of his fingers...Owch.

When we arrive, we are greeted with the young man grinning his teeth, rocking back and forth in his seat. We unravel the remainder of the finger and take a look, it's not a clean cut, instead its uneven and cut at an angle. I ask him where the missing part of his finger is and he replies, 'In the shed somewhere', So with my mentor cleaning the wound, I pop out to the shed and have a look.

'Found it!', I say, as I appear back in the room with an extra finger in my hand!

I drop it inside a large syringe to take with us to ED, they will want to X-ray it to check if there is any bone before attempting to re-attach it.

Back to school

In between placement blocks, we returned to university where we had assignments and presentations to work on. These included topics such as Mental health, Practice education, Pathophysiology and Critical thinking. Alongside reflections from practice and building a PAD portfolio which we will build and add too over the years to (hopefully) impress future employers.

At the beginning, I could not get my head around essay writing. My feedback from my first ever draft had every second sentence highlighted with comments such as 'Who wrote this?' 'Who said this?', and my reply was a very confused...'Me?... I'm saying this?', I was then taught the importance of referencing. Pain in the arse is what it is. You can't have an opinion unless you can find someone else who had that same opinion before you, so you can reference them as 'evidence'.

Who made these rules, anyway?

I soon got the hang of writing essays and I gave myself plenty of time to complete each, most universities will allow you to submit a draft or two to receive feedback before final submission, I found this helpful, in making sure I am on the right lines for each essay. There is also additional support available through most libraries, which can offer advice on essays amongst everything else.

For me, I work better on a laptop or an actual computer, but I did start off the year with an iPad and keyboard, which I ended up selling.

Think about which works best for you, I work faster on my laptop than on my iPad, especially on essays.

Some people are a whiz with technology, making pretty notes on tablets. I'm still a big fan of a good pen and paper, which is what I used for my note taking in class, I would write rough notes then expand and make them pretty, before organizing into files, but that's just me. So just think what's best for you to work on before you make any purchases.

As the months go by, we are taking on more and more knowledge and skills responsibilities. We start looking at reading ECG's (tracings of the heart), Needle work (Cannulation, etc). ALS (Advanced life support), Drugs and greater system assessments.

I recommend getting a good ECG book or an app on your phone which explains ECG's and common findings. You will find that no two ECG's are the same, so honestly, look at as many as you can get your hands on and try breaking it down into sections.

With our skills suitcase expanding, the pressure was on to perfect these skills in practice, first on mannequins and plastic arms... but soon, on real life human beings.

I thrive in pressure, and I really enjoy having extra responsibility thrown at me. I like to prove myself. So, I was keen to take all my new knowledge and skills into practice, and soon enough... it was time to don the green uniform once again.

Adult female in cardiac arrest.

This job comes through and we are literally around the corner, we switch on the blue lights and watch the traffic split to the side of the road and let us through. On approach to the scene, I recognize the area, I've seen groups of people sit on this bench each time I pass, often drinking or sleeping rough. There's a handful of people gathered, and one bystander is giving mouth to mouth.

As this is my first arrest, my adrenaline is pumping. I grab the bags and jump off. Myself, my mentor & the emergency care assistant (ECA) on duty today each take our own role, as though we had rehearsed one hundred times. The paramedic attaches the de-fib, the ECA takes over chest compressions, and I open the airway bag and prepare an I-GEL for insertion. I give the woman breaths using a thing called a BVM (Bag valve mask), then I place the I-GEL in her throat. If you are wondering what the heck an I-GEL is, Google it, or ask Alexa. The lady is in her mid 30's. She had injected heroin and immediately collapsed and stopped breathing. Her groupies are watching, 'I've put the needles away', one says. Assuming they have been using as well, one is hysterical, screaming 'WHAT AM I SEEING', Then another is a chilled as anything, sunbathing on the bench and nursing a bottle of some cheap looking booze.

Another paramedic turns up and joins us, we deliver shocks and drugs to try and revive this woman. I am focusing on my job, delivering air into the lungs to allow everything to circulate inside. Time feels like its still, I look at this lady, she is real. I have practiced this exact situation so many times, but this one... is real. I look up, her stomach... she is pregnant.

Normally we would stay on scene until we have a reason to stop, either the heart starts working again or else we all agree to stop and pronounce the person dead. But not this time, we were minutes away from the hospital, so we scoop the lady onto a stretcher and into the back of the ambulance. We have now all swapped roles and I am preforming chest compressions. I am surprised as it feels easier on a real person than on a mannequin.

We roll into resus and the team there take over.

I step back, peel off my gloves (which are dripping with sweat) and bring myself back down to earth as I wash my hands. We take our time restocking the truck and debriefing after.

A few weeks pass and we follow up on the lady with staff at ED. Turns out she recovered, but self-discharged herself from hospital 2 weeks later, unfortunately... the same thing happened again, but she didn't make it that time.

'Man laying on driveway.'

One summers day, we are called to a wheelchair user who was found laying on his driveway. His neighbour has called when he heard shouting from over the fence.

We arrive and the crew I'm with recognize the man right away, he's a frequent caller. An alcoholic. He has had numerous ambulances out earlier in the past 24 hours for numerous reasons. But none the less, he is on the floor and needs our assistance.

I introduce myself and the crew. 'Get me off this f**king floor, you c****'. Nice bloke.

I explain we are preparing our lifting cushion which will help him. I try to find out how he has ended up on the ground, but he isn't making much sense in his drunken state. To make matters worse, he is lay in dog poo.

I check him over for any injuries, he is fine. As we fix his chair up and get him off the ground, we ask if he would like to come to hospital to be checked out. He declines and instead wishes to be pushed into his house, we comply.

As I step inside, I take a look around the house, it's a shell of a home. There is nothing but a hospital bed in the lounge, and an old TV.

The toilet (with no door) is filled to the rim with urine and whatever else, however the bucket in the corner of the lounge tells me he doesn't even use said toilet.

As we are about to leave, he decides he now wants to go to hospital. No problem, we get him out as far as the driveway, I shut the door behind me.

'No, I'm not going to fe*king hospital, take me back in!' – he scolds.

After a deep breath, and an attempt to open the door I've just closed... I realise we cannot get back in. It's one of those key only locks with no handle on the outside. Shit.

'Ahh.. we can't go back in, Do you have a key?', I ask.

He doesn't...says he usually leaves the door open all the time.

Great.

After a brief discussion, we let control know we will be breaking the door, and to send the police around later to patch it up. Finally inside the man is happy and content to stay at home.

We leave before he can change his mind again.

Down time.

I suppose I should explain what happens in between call outs now. Let's start with the beginning of shift, the tucks or car is checked and wiped down, we restock equipment, do a defib check, as well as check oxygen tanks and battery levels of equipment. Once that is done, we let control know we are all set and then we wait.

This time is really valuable as a student, you have time to spend getting to know your mentor and crew that day, make an impression, ask questions and express what you would like to achieve if you get the opportunity. This is also a good time to go over some reflections on previous jobs and get any signatures you may need.

On station, there is usually a lounge area, as well as a TV room and kitchen area, at the very least. We kick back, flick through the TV, and await the bleep of the radio to deliver us a job.

In between jobs, if there are none outstanding when we clear, we may be sent to a standby position or asked to return to station. On the way back to station, we often make an excuse to fuel up on Tesco meal deals, honestly, - what a bargain they are.

Through a 12-hour shift, we are entitled lunch break then a further evening break. There is a certain window / time frame which when you enter, you are protected until you get back to station. By protected I mean that you should not get any calls through unless they are Category 1, the most urgent call and if you are the nearest vehicle. If we don't get time to take our evening break, we get to finish half an hour earlier, and if you finish your shift late... you are entitled to start your next shift late, to allow the 11 hour gap in between shifts.

You might be surprised to hear that a busy day in the life of an ambulance, may only see 5 or 6 patients.

It's one of the things I really like about the role, not that I don't want to see a whole load of patients, but because when we do see a patient... they receive our full undivided attention. We spend as long is as needed on scene with a patient, before deciding what to do with them. We do not have other people forming an orderly que nor do we have a patient across the hallway shouting for a bedpan, the patient in front of us is our main and only focus (Unless there is a major incident or multiple casualty ofcourse).

On a few occasions, when we have turned up at a patient's house, you would be surprised how many times family members think this entitles them to a full health check MOT too.

'Oh, since you're here... could you just look at this for me, it's itchy and it smells...'

> Wow wow wow, let us stop you there... We only deal with one person at a time missy, get yourself to your GP.

Police custody – Patient, unconscious.

We've just came of our lunch break and a category 1 call comes through from a police custody unit nearby. We go on blues. I'm interested to see what the job is, and also what the inside of a prison looks like. I've heard crew members talk about the high security checks they've had to go through before entering prisons for call outs. We approach the building and the shutter lifts to allow us entry. Once inside we are enclosed in, like a huge garage. Shutter in and shutter out. I lift the bags and we're greeted by an officer to let us inside. It's exactly as I imagined. Grey concrete, thick, battered steel doors. We are led through the booking in desk and into their Nurses room. We meet a prison nurse and her patient, an 'unconscious' man. One look at this man tells me he isn't unconscious at all. The nurse explains that this man was arrested for shop lifting, he was pulled over after being flagged from witness description and was also found to be intoxicated behind the wheel. She explains he became 'unresponsive' whilst being questioned. She tested his blood sugar levels, which read HIGH. The patient previously mentioned that he is diabetic and he has also been drinking, which contributes to his sugars being high. This is known as hyperglycemia and can cause unconsciousness in severe case, however... we say 'Let's get you to the ambulance and check you out', and the man stands up and walks out with us. He has either forgot he is 'unconscious' or he is happy to get what he has planned, a trip to A&E and a delay in supplying a breath specimen.

On board, the man takes a comfy lay down on our trolley, we carry out our observations and I cannulate him to administer fluids. He closes his eyes and doesn't say a word.

The police escort, one officer with us and a car following. The man is not only hand cuffed but also strapped into our trolley bed. As we buckle ourselves in, I offer the police lady to sit as there is 3 seats available in the back. She declines and chooses to stand for the journey. Too cool for the law of a seatbelt? Must be.

Your questions answered

Now on the topic of seatbelts, let's talk about driving.

Driving is an essential part of being a Paramedic. The biggest insult to anyone in the ambulance service is 'Oh you're an ambulance driver then'. Idiots.

I think with most universities, you will need to hold a normal drivers licence before you begin, however not with all uni's, so again...do the research.

I would strongly recommend getting your licence before you begin your course, as honestly, I don't think the additional stress and funding of lessons would be worth it on top of your course. Plus, when placement starts, shifts often start really early, or awkward times to be using public transport, and you could be placed up to an hour away from your address.

Ofcourse then, there is the addition C1 category needed to enable you to drive an ambulance.

For me, I completed this at the beginning of my third year, but the process took around a year due to corona-virus.

I applied for my provisional C1 at the beginning of second year, for this, I needed to complete a form and a medical check from a GP, this cost me £110.

Once completed and sent off, I had to wait up to 12 weeks for my licence to return, before I was able to book my theory. I downloaded the official UK Driving theory app and used that for study, it cost around £5 to download but I found it really helpful.

Finally, after passing my theory, I was in a position to book lessons and practical test for C1. This is the most expensive part, costing around £600-£1000 depending on different companies. I done a bit of research and went with a company who offered two days lessons with the test on the third day, for £650.

A costly but necessary addition.

I have had a lot of people ask, if it is possible to hold a part time job whilst studying an intense course like this. The answer is yes, it is totally do-able! (I'm speaking as a single person with no kids).

I have held down 2 bank contract jobs throughout the course of my degree. Bank contracts means 0 hours, you get to pick and choose your hours around what suits you. If you can prioritise your time well, let your employer know that you require flexibility, then there is nothing stopping you doing a few hours each week. Ofcourse, if you have children and childcare to consider, your situation is different. But, I know some super mum's on my course who have been single parents throughout, and it does not slow them from the rest!

I tend to take on more shifts in the evenings and weekends during term time to put some money away for during placement blocks. Trust me, working will be the last thing you will want to do after completing 40+ hours of placement each week.

I recommend checking with your local hospital advertising for Healthcare assistants. This a great job to gain extra experience and exposure to patients and medical environments. I gained so much experience from this job and got to speak to staff in every field, they have always been helpful and open to questioning whenever they know you are a medical student as well.

I particularly enjoyed picking up shifts in A&E, this allowed me a greater insight into the care and treatment patients receive after the ambulance drops them off.

During our second year of the course we were allocated some hospital shifts as placement experience. These were to maternity, A&E and theatres, I found this a really enjoyable placement which allowed me to observe numerous intubations and even a thyroidectomy!

As the end of year two approached, the final placement block of the year saw us out in the winter months. On top of ambulance shifts, we prepped for a pharmacology exam and developed a dissertation proposal which is to be expanded on in third year.

'What's the worst job you've ever seen?'

Well...

'Have you ever seen a man eat his own hand?

Me either.

That is such a fragile question I would think most people in the ambulance service dread. As if they would want to recall the most traumatic image, they have probably spent months storing deep at the back of their mind, for you to stand with your mouth open.

I once asked a para this, and the response I got was that they scraped a persons remains off a train track.
What do you say to that? You wish you didn't ask in the first place.

I can't tell you the worst job I've been too, but I can tell you my favorite, so far.

Baby girl

On a day shift and I am working from my usual station, but with a newly qualified paramedic. We are on our way to a 'Abdo pain' when we get diverted to a 'Woman In labour'. I'm excited as I may get to experience my first birth. I try not to get my hopes up too much, as I've been to a few 'labour' calls already and we always manage to get them to hospital before any babies make an appearance.

The radio goes off and it is control telling us the baby has been born but is breathing ineffectively.

My excitement turns to adrenaline and I pick up all the equipment as soon as we stop. The mum's friend meets us outside and leads us to a top floor apartment.
Mum is standing in the hallway; baby is in her arms wrapped in a jumper.

I take baby from mum and begin to rub her to stimulate breathing, she cries. A welcomed sound.

We swaddle baby in a clean towel, blankets and a little hat. Her temperature is low, and her tiny arms and legs are a shade of grey. We clamped the umbilical cord and mum offers her friend to cut it.

(The maternity packs on the ambulance contain everything you need, a clean towel, hat, clamp and scissors. Perfect for those unexpected babies!)

There is a sense of relief in the room, that everything is going to be ok. Mum is good too, she has made it look easy! She was laughing and joking with her friend. I hand baby back to mum who places her on her chest. I feel privileged to be part of this moment.

We offered mum some pain relief and waited for her to deliver the placenta.

A back up crew arrived, 2 lady staff who both had experience delivering babies, they knew what to do next. They phoned ahead to the hospital and explained the midwifes the arrival of this baby girl.

They confirmed to bring mum & baby in, and they would assess the two of them.

As I wash my hands at the hospital, I can't help but smile. What an amazing experience. Being the first to hold this little baby who was only minutes old.

I am on a high for the rest of that shift.

Toilet talk.

One thing I have learnt, and I will stress, to anyone entering this job...

Use the toilet when you have a chance!! Even if you think you can hold it, use the hospital facilities, the station, or the nice fancy house, when you have a chance.

I learnt this the hard way. We had been on a few call outs, and in between calls, I had been sipping on my water bottle. And an orange juice, and a squash.

I realised I really needed a wee when we are completing paperwork from our previous job. I begin typing out a message to control... 'Need to use facilities, going to the fuel garage', but I as I went to press send, a job comes through.

'Chest pain'

This can't be ignored. 'Ok', I say, 'let's hope they have a toilet.'

We arrive at a coach type house, there is work going on to the outer part of the building and we have difficulty finding the entrance. The patient opens the door and before we can exchange hellos, I ask to use his toilet. 'Sure,' he says, and directs me into the bathroom.

I step inside the bathroom and my hand reaches for the door to shut it behind me.

Trouble is, there is no door.

I look around in confusion... still no door. Instead, a makeshift curtain hung on a line. I debate for a second if I can avoid this situation or not, but I can't.

I pull the curtain and finally have my wee. I pray that my mentor and the patient can't hear my flow as they are just outside the room.

Lesson learnt.

Always. Use. The. Toilet.

'Adult male, cardiac arrest'

It's a sunny winters day and we're admiring the scenery on the drive back from a job. We receive a call through, 'Adult male in cardiac arrest'. Blue lights on, we follow the sat nav to our destination.

We find a bit of a delay as the location is in remote countryside and is difficult to access.

As we arrive, HEMs are on scene (Helicopter crew), preforming CPR. We join them, introduce ourselves and they allocate us jobs, we take over the ventilations and prepare drugs. They have a device called a LUCAS which preforms chest compressions on the patient. It's an amazing device and I question why all ambulances do not carry them. It allows an extra set of hands free to do other tasks.

It is explained to us that the man collapsed whilst out walking, and had bystander CPR straight away - this is good and increases the chance of survival.

I watch the HEMs team in awe. I admire how in sync they are and how they seem like they could do this with their eyes closed.

The doctor allows me space to cannulate the patient and he then administers the drugs. The patient's heart is in an abnormal rhythm and he has received several shocks to try and restart his heart back into a regular rhythm. It eventually works, we attach our monitoring equipment and I retrieve the trolley bed from the truck. The patient then re-arrests and the LUCAS machine is switched on again. We go back and forth a few times before his heart starts again.

After what feels like forever, the HEMs doctors decide to move the man onto the helicopter and get him to the hospital. The have intubated him, meaning they can now continue circulating oxygen around his body whilst they move him to hospital.

We spend time on scene after they leave, to clean up, and debrief. It still shocks me how quick death occurs, to be alive and doing something you enjoy one minute, to being clinically dead the next. It's the little things, like the man's phone, ringing in his pocket, that hits home with me. Someone is calling him, someone is expecting him to answer, no one is expecting this.

'Scooter accident'

The city has introduced E-scooters that can be accessed and rode around down on a 'pay as you go' basis.

A fun way to travel, you might think. But to healthcare staff, these just scream RISK.

First of all, they don't come with helmets.

Secondly, they go up to 30 mph,

Thirdly, there's no helmets?!?

Several calls come in throughout the night, of incidents involving these scooters. Stories of two people on one scooter, ends in a disaster, one gets off lightly with minor injuries, the other is transferred to a major hospital with a bleed in the brain.

My call is to a male in his 30's found unconscious on the road after colliding with car, whilst on the scooter.

As we approach the man regains consciousness, he is laying in a pool of his own blood and there is a massive opening on the front of his head. He has darted the car windscreen, and I will say it again, with no helmet!

I apply pressure to the open wound and support his neck as he could have a serious C-spine injury. My collegues get the scoop board and head blocks so we can lift this man onto our trolley bed.

Once in the ambulance, we bandage his head to apply more pressure, in the space of a few minutes his head has swollen to the point he now looks like a mushroom. He doesn't complain, he is intoxicated. He makes light conversation.

We are only minutes from ED and when we get him on to a bed, we have the job of cleaning up the puddles of blood brought in with our patient. There are giant clotted pools of blood on the floor, and dripping from our trolley bed, like jellyfish.

I check back on the patient later when we are back in ED, he seemed to be doing ok and was more concerned about his favorite shirt being ruined, people are funny!

The end, for now.

As I move into my final year, I will focus on leadership and facilitating learning, management of trauma, minor illness and injuries as well as driving change in practice.

I can't believe how fast the years have gone and to imagine the next step is to be fully out on the road, as a shiny new Paramedic, possibly mentoring students of my own!
I feel ready, I am keen to get going, but for now... I will enjoy squeezing every opportunity I can out of both university and personal experiences.

I want to thank, all the amazing healthcare workers, who are working tirelessly to treat people during this difficult time. I have witnessed firsthand, the struggle and effort put in by all, and I have never been prouder of a career, than the one I am about to embark on.

And finally,
I wish you all the best, on your journey.

Printed in Great Britain
by Amazon

32552259R00059